The Boy in the Ring

The Boy in the Ring
Dave Lordan

salmonpoetry

Published in 2007 by
Salmon Poetry,
Cliffs of Moher, County Clare, Ireland
Website: www.salmonpoetry.com
Email: info@salmonpoetry.com

ISBN 978-1-903392-60-7

Cover artwork: 'Jester on a white horse' by Dave Lordan
Cover design & typesetting: Siobhán Hutson

for my mother and father Joe and Mary Lordan

Burn like a fire
Burn like a fire in Cairo
Flare with a wonderful light
Like a fire in Cairo

Fire In Cairo — The Cure

Acknowledgments

Grateful acknowledgement to the editors of the following publications where some of these poems first appeared: *The Stinging Fly, Poetry Ireland Review, Poetry Ireland News, The Irish Examiner, Metro Eireann, Socialist Worker, Al Quds Al Arabi, The Internationalist Review of Irish Culture, An Crannog, Citizen 32, Poetry Kit, Nthposition, Catullus Reactie, Poetryfish, Arabesques, Blackmail Press, Deficit, New .Verse News, The Handstand, Streetnotes, SAW, Eyewear.*

The poems 'Driving Home From Derry', 'My Country', 'Explanations of War', 'Holding Chirac's Hand in Temple Bar', 'The Longest Queue' appeared in the anthology *Unoccupied Minds* published by the Irish Anti War Movement.

The poem 'Love' appeared in the anthology *Babylon Burning* published by nthposition.

I would like to thank the Arts Council/An Comhairle Ealaion for the generous bursary granted to me in 2004

Thanks to Gerald Dawe and Brendan Kennelly and my classmates on the M.Phil. in Creative Writing Course in The Oscar Wilde Centre in Trinity College, Dublin.

I would especially like to thank Roisin and Louise Berg for the biscuits and the forest walks in Mountshannon, Co Clare, while I was working on this collection.

Thanks for encouragement, support and inspiration to John Costello, Peadar O Grady, Danny Friel, Janette Griffin, Charlie K, Gavin and Camilla, Tom Coughlan, Melisa Halpin, Peter Sheekey, Treasa Ahern, Ciara Hogan, Annie Tanner, Eamonn McGrath, Nicola Coleman, Ciarán and Ann, Esso, Emer, Sanya Barber, Joe Woods, Maureen and Denis, Garrett Lordan, Helena, Sinéad, the Ryders, Paula, Aidan and Jessie, Joe and Heather, Eamonn and Leah, Nick, Tommy, Juvo and all upstairs in Monkstown, JP, Josh, Christy, Hugh, Shay, Gino, Doreen, Teabags, Brian C, Ruth, Brendan O D, Caroline, Eoin, Carolann, Orla, Declan, Dave C, Michael, Billy, Frank, Flora, Jools, Kevin and Susan, John, Miceal, Brendan, Stephen, Neil, Ray, Elaine, Jack, John, Hugh, Trish, Rosa, Denis Redfern, Milan Lucic.

Contents

At Oscar Wilde's Grave

Who stole the angel's glory?
Still, you've got the rarest grave in Montparnasse,
Granite teeming with lipstick kisses,
A shoal of petals in a mountain lake,
A cloud burst of tropical fish,
And taped to a withering rose there's a note:
Thank you for teaching me that I was good.

I kiss the teacher too
For you are more than welcome
To the imprint of my gaping mouth
If I can stay awhile in reverence
To watch my wet gift fading,
November sun licking my lips.

The Boy in the Ring

Where is the boy?
The boy is in the ring.
And where is the ring?
The ring is in the school-yard.
And what makes up the ring?
The ring is made of other boys.

What kind is this ring?
It is a spinning ring, and a jeering ring
a hissing ring
a rhyming ring
a kicking ring
a spitting ring
a teeth, tongue and eyelid ring, a hair and eyes ring
a snot and nostrils ring, a knee and knuckles ring
a fist and boot and mouth and ear and elbow ring.

Who is the god of this ring?
The god of the ring is unknown.
Jack O the Lantern maybe
or the scarecrow with the two axes
or a wailing midnight wind
or a sack of smashed glass.

What is the boy doing in the ring?
The boy is looking
at himself in the ring.

He is sitting down
and crying
and looking at himself
in the ring.

Why did the boy go into the ring?
The boy never went into the ring.

When will the boy get out of the ring?

Today John Lennon will die

Cold enough for gloves.
A sky the colour of tripe
clings to Clonakilty's rooftops.
Our two spires hide in fog.

At school we warm our fingers
twisting little figures out of mála,
the last flecks of rainbow congealing
into shit-brown as we roll.

At small break the big boys beat
the babies up. At big break
they beat us up again. My belly hurts.
Mrs Crowley scolds *"Only Cows Have Bellies"*.

At home a young woman is suddenly old.
She stretches on the settee weeping.
A man on the telly keeps standing up and falling over,
standing up and falling over.

A few bob short

Just a few bob son, if you're carryin, an' we'll see you the next day.
Tellin you again how well the German's used pay out
how the weekends and the nights were double-time,
treble over if you worked a holiday,
how you'd only be scratchin yerself the half of it
but once you kept an eye out you were fine.

The way t'was all functions an' outins.
Dunmore house hired out for the Christmas,
oul Paddy Nolan, god rest him, as Santy,
and a sack full of presents for the kids.
They got the turkey and ham, sherry trifle after,
mints an' cigars, any drink they might fancy.

Or about that time the 'pool were playin away in Portugal,
the little chat he'd had with Beckenbauer,
(to his face they called him Mr Heinkel, his real name).
Don't go askin him how or who had fixed it
but didn't Heinkel go an' charter 'em a jumbo jet
an' book three hundred tickets for the game.

In Lisbon they'd wallets fat as millionaires
and the beer was weak as piss and cheap as water.
Some lads'd be in deep shit with their wives
if half what they got up to travelled home,
three whole days they spent as drunk as lords
an' the quare ones all over them like flies.

Now, it's only half way through the long slump
of a Tuesday afternoon. You're getting laughter
from the lounge bar but it's canned.
He's sucking the arse out of a Johnny Blue.
His glass is damn near empty. He's a few bob short.
On his mother's life you'll get it back into your hand.

A Game of Donkey

It's Christmastime in Matty Googan's pub.
The men are all brothers.
The women in love.
The kids have been sitting on Santy.
All are merry having fun .

The boy finds a ring in his lucky bag
and the grown-ups start playing a game.

They're making a ring
around a man and his wife.

She's pretending to be a stubborn donkey
down on all fours and braying.

He's the ass's owner in a hurry,
kicking it in the belly,
and dragging it along by the mane.

Scrobbers

For Leo Flynn

Tread quiet now boys
all in line
down the boreen

Step soft
on the whip of grass

For a stray foot-fall
on that sun-leatherned muck

Or a pebble kicked
off a can in the ditch

Or even so much
as a cracked twig

Would set the wild dogs
to warning

And draw the farmer down
out of his stony house

With his screeching wife
and his two blind sons

And a bloody fine end
then
they'd make of us

With a scythe
and a shovel
and an oul shot gun.

The Ear

Like a canine embryo in a chemical dye
like a burst calf's lip
like snails in wine
like a bleeding purse

the bitten ear
setting in its blood
on the white stripe
in the middle of the road

the man with the sovvie rings
cupping his hands
to the gouting cavity
in the side of his head

did not ask the boy for help
doesn't need his towel
or his basin of salty water

Fishing Trip in Gatsby's

After a while leaning out over the balcony railing
and peering down
through strobes and dry ice
at the dance-floor
swarming with underage drunks
you swim back towards your seat
quizzing yourself:
now that I have put my fist through the jukebox
and the sleeve of my finest white shirt
is a sponge of blood
what is the worst?
Are these people whirling beneath me
or are they only fish?
Are they only fish
gagging to be netted
And gutted by the bucketful?
And do fish have feelings?

You'll answer these riddles in Gatsby's tonight.
A fish or two will tell
how much or not it hurts

Though you'll goof for a while
on the way
the rotating lights warp
like spooky luminous fish
in a bowl
on the fat jags of a smashed pint-bottle

before flipping it over your shoulder
into the shòal

Fearless

Fearless
I'm fuckin fearless
Try me now why don't ya
An' I promise ya faithfully
Ya won't last too long

Cos I'm the wan they're all on about
When they're drinkin their fuckin coffee
Above in Sullivan's café
Yeh I'm the wan that ripped the fag machine
Down off the wall above in Bernie's lounge

I'm the likes that spreads meself out on a bench
Above in the square of a summer's day
Suckin a flagon with me shirt tore off an' me pot belly out
Fuckin an' blindin anyone who'd be passin
Tellin dem I'm fearless fuckin fearless

Last Friday I got shteamed above in Cork
Got fucked outta Henry's for bitin some youngfella's ear off
Well as I was passin out beyond the viaduct
I got a mad tashpie to run out on the road
An' I screamin into the headlights how I'm fearless fuckin fearless

I'm the laziest oul bollox that ever you met
But I'd ate your fuckin eyeballs in a shot
I'm barred from every pub in town an' every bookies too
But I'd walk to Tipperary for a drink an' a bet
Yeh I'd walk to Tipperary for a drink an' a bet

Cos I'm fearless
Fuckin fearless
Don't believe me?

Doubt me now?
Watch me go so

Till I stick a pint glass into me brow
An' lepp up onto the counter like a pure fuckin tiger
An' kick the heads wan by wan off the beer taps
And I watchin meself in the big bar mirror
As I dance in the blood an' the fountains o' beer
Yeh as I dance in the blood an' the fountains o' beer

Ode on de winning of de Entente Florale

For Joseph Lordan and Sammy Tanner

Told ye so. Told ye we could win it
'Spite de filth o' de likes o' ye
With yere baseball caps and yere baggy pants,
Yere ghetto blasters and yere nigger music,
Yere flagons and yere Mitsoobeachies [*],
And de trainee hoors hangin' offa ye.

Rollin in muck ye are, de flays atin' ye.
Manged an' stinkin like tinkers' mares
like yere faaders and mudders before ye,
but I'd say yere not too sure who bore ye;
Shir who pished you out Twishty? De milkman?
De coalman? One o' Fossetts' weepin clowns?

This here's 'come a champion little town
all down to good people like me.
We've patched every crack with vines,
blossoms cover every stain. Tis like paradise,
'ceptin ye, ye shnakes, ye divils, ye dirty filthy
feckin animals. Ye give us all a bad name.

[*] Mitsubishis are a brand of E

In the Model Village

We're not being smart
Tom Thumb *is* our blacksmith
we've a dozen Spinning Jennys here on loan from Lilliput
the Sly Fella's calling to arms from the back of a lorry
the length of a shoebox
the Big Fella and his penny farthing
would fit in your pocket

There's a rosy six inch Irish maiden for you
collecting plastic apples in our knee-high forest
mind don't step on Molly Malone's first cousin
and she hawking a basket of plasticine salmon

We're not supposed to use the church spire for leaning
but it's handy for an elbow-rest when you're smoking
and the nave is just the right height and angle
for comfortable sitting

And believe me
if we needed to
or were ever asked
we could easily dismantle the brewery
stamp on the charnel house
kick in the workhouses' walls
flatten the schools and the barracks
trample the cotton mills into the ground

We'd go down on all fours
and like the big bad wolves
we'd huff and we'd puff
till the whole of Pearse Street
and Emmett Square were just whirling smithereens

but we're not that dangerous or threatening
and we never were truly
one good sweep of a yard brush
would clear away our part in the rising
and we're at least fifteen score miles
and three generations away
from the slightest need
for TNT

Instead, when we're suspended
in the long dying
of an August afternoon
between a busload of Spanish artillerymen
and a troop of Korean nuns
we pore over *Lonely Planets*
and *Rough Guides*
and Philip's maps of the universe
plotting our autumn's escapes
to the never-ending highs
in Shane McGowan's Siam

When the gulf stream is flowing royally in
to occupy Inchadoney bay
and the cavalier breeze with its muskets of sand
its acids and powders of citrus and flesh
is blasting the stink of ancient shite away
then us summer guides can count
on making it through
to our various starlit elopements
to the rainbows of the moon

While we're waiting
we're here and at your service
we'll give you the essence of four hundred years
in fifteen learned off paragraphs
and recite the short story of how

our settlement grew on a stone in the wood
tripped over a long time ago
by a very minor Tudor

That's our miniature town in a nutshell
that's our model village for you
do come and visit sir and don't forget
to bring along your friends
you know very well Clonakilty's future depends
on the kindness of giants like you

so God be with you sir
and God's blessings on your wife and family
and God help us.

Mail for a dead guide

Dear ——
my friend and fellow guide
green-shirted puppet just like me
It's been a long time
and a lot of shite has been spewing into the bay
since were dossing together
in the Model Village.

Forgive me my intrusion on your peace.
(I guess its you whose been fiddling with the TV and the lights).

I needed to let you know
I've been looking back
trying to figure out what exactly happened
to us
and to me
and I'm pretty sure
it was our tininess
our lack of *power*
that finished you.

I remember the afternoon you were told
you'd failed the August exams.
Now mom and dad
would be taking a scissors
to the pocket strings
and the wide panorama of your life
had suddenly zoomed
to a puppet show in a shoe box.
So it was straight on the lock after work
straight to the cider and chasers
till six hours and ten pints later,
speechlessly locked,

you tottered from your stool
to a raggy heap
on the pukey sawdust in the Fiddler's Green.

What a howl! We were nearly split!
Then we pulled you up and slapped you off
and continued downing pints
till September drew its tawny blinds
around our summer cabaret.

Then it was good bye good luck and see you next June
as we all flew away in a whirl
to College balls and all night parties
or to summer's second coming in Australia.

Left behind to tread the mulch
and lick the drizzle from your lips
you kept on boozing all alone
falling and falling again
falling and falling back down
into your own hollowness
into the paralysis of an uncast marionette

while winter sped towards you darkening
in the massive shadow of a hand
stretching down through the ceiling
to shuffle you around
the mouldy stage to Tipperary

where a human factory tried shrinking you
to the dimensions of the fake smile
in the photograph on your CV
trying to melt you down
and filter out your elemental care and gentleness
stir you dizzy with their nightsticks
in their butchers' vat

bubbling with gristle and blood and fat
mix you up in wigs and sirens and harps
boil you senseless
along with warrants and certificates and stamps
pour and stretch you stiffening
into a quota
into a uniform
but you would not fit.

I know
that according to our village scriptures
we shouldn't be talking.
I know they'll carp I have salt in my eyes and know nothing
for sure I'm only speculating
but, meaning no offense to you and yours,
I do believe
it was because
you wouldn't harden to their mould

that you went out
that January day
deep
into the forest's changeling ground
so nakedly

and slipped yourself into a knot
on the bark of an oak
disappearing out of their diminishing vision
completely.

Cureheads

For Danny

In the realm of the shit-kickers
and the rabbit punchers
and the head butters
during the terrible five year reign
of the flying gang of ear chewing brothers
with metallers getting stuck into ravers
and coppers getting stuck into travellers
with the Rossmore Hackers
whipping the seven varieties of shite out
of the Bandon Boy racers
and with all the magnificent Saturday samurai
all the capsizing warriors' legendary names in the bloody spit
and bloody snot
running into the puke and the piss
                        and the half eaten burgers

The pair of of us behind the vines
hanging down from the sleepers re-used
as beams for a walkway
at the back of the Chateaulin gardens
sucking our joints and our flagons
with the convent girls we were aiding to cheat on their parents,
Treassa and Tara, Maeve and Deirdre and Grainne,
all supping and inhaling in turns and fits
of lebanese giggles at our panda black eyelids,
our brazen red lips, our defiantly moony-white pusses;
we were gorgeously freakish
and spitting out midges
while spouting of truth and of love and nausea with
quotes from the ur-texts:
Disintegration, The Head on The Door
Pornography, Seventeen Seconds, Kiss Me Kiss Me Kiss Me

Please also remind me of Augusts
famously twisted in spidery corners
of Fahey's, De Barra's and Fiddlers
on snakebites and smuggled-in naggins,
how when the Soldiers of Destiny rose all at once in the
cross drafts
at TIME NOW GENTLEMEN PLEASE
to drive the British out of Ireland with their thumbnails
we held our position, we stayed in our seats.
Was that not risk of life and limb?
Was that not courage?
Was that not brotherhood?

I recall being packed in a 747
among row upon row of dead uncles
and flown three thousand miles home
where, by my illegal dying, taboo in my room
big bully shame had me under the blankets,
bully boy shame had me pinned to the mattress,
and no-one would call to my door for fear of infection,
for fear I would lead them down tunnels and wells,
for fear I would lead them to forests of wolves.

That was bleak mid-winter
and I was unwell and alone.
I could not conceive of a future.

Then you were standing before me
brushing your fringe from your forehead,
all sleepy and slurred and glazed over,
GP'd to the rim of your senses like me
in a sweater three sizes too big,
thumbs through the holes in the sleeves,
black denims, basketball boots trailing white laces,
enormous purple tongues flopping over your pull-ups,

having swung your way through to my door
to hack me out of the silence
to open your mouth, smile, and enquire *How's it goin'?*,
spread your woolly wings out and embrace me,
be alone out of all of the living
and reach out and touch me.

Grace Day

There are mummies made of seaweed
along Inchadoney's shore.

White are their bandages,
green their spilled life.

We saw them on a Grace Day,
me and my wife.

We saw them
and we knew who they were.

Green are the bandages,
white the spilled life.

There are mummies made of seaweed
along Inchadoney's shore.

Tea

All night long
I've been listening to his racket,
now Uncle Georgie's making tea again,
same craic every night of his week old visit,
home alone from lonely London.

First loose slip-ons slapping the lino
then the handle rattling on the kitchen door,
rusty scraping of a lock, hinges slowly creaking open,

Again,
again I hear a switch being flicked,
sugar crunch, tea leaves shaken,
the kettle spout its whistling hiss,
teaspoon and cup
ring out like a bell.

Bath

What is this place he's landed in
a thousand miles from home?
his white tin box, his Holloway cot,
his hermit's cell, a coffin's length, in his sister's flat,
where he lies down at night, a guest of the dead,
gathering all the secrets of this house,
from belching pipes and gurgling drains,
from scuttling mice and the boiler's ticks,
from dripping taps and the baby's whelps,
unwinding in draughts flowing under the door
to the muffled groans of a thousand ghosts.

His bath-bed, his rack, his cage of knit tusks
a shark's jaw-bone, skeleton's eye-hole,
white as a surgical sheet, where he wakes, if he wakes,
his limbs clamped with aches,
a numbness etched into his flesh,
no sense in his fingers or feet.
Where all through the night
the seeds of his fear bloom abortions
that like claws in his throat won't let him talk,
like glass in his gut won't let him eat,
like bricks on his back won't let him rise.

His bath-raft, his bone-boat, shuttle, his moon-cone
where he, like Major Tom,
drifts far from the needle points of stars
in utter darkness a thousand years from home,
and dreams, if he dreams, of coasting down
the arches of the nebulae back to his time's beginning
in a parish saved from lightening
where rainbows bud from open palms
and his mother drones her only air

I'm riding along in a free train
bound for nobody knows where.

*

a mans eyes cry a boy's tears
a thousand miles a thousand years
a thousand ghosts from home

what he needs so he won't dream
the miles he won't fear the years
he won't feel the ghosts he won't hear

of home what he needs so at last
he will sleep what he needs
is a drink is a drink is a drink

Kilburn Bridewell, 1967

1

Bawled awake on a slab o' granite
In de arsehole of a Bridewell

Reek like a slaughterhouse truck
Trousers damp an' stuck to me legs

Throat like I swalleed tar
A chip from me front tooth, lips o' dried puke

A pain in de curl o' me brow
Like a Kango tunnellin out

2

Recall no sort o' incident
Only went to wet de lips after work

Dere was fiddles an' whoopin
Fine lookin women an' a plate o' puddin

Den black like I fell down a manhole
Like I got swalleed by a whale

Black like de dark o' de womb
De dark hours whooshed into a vacuum

3

Desk Sergeant hands over me shoes an' me keys
Presents me with fog on a charge sheet.

Sign here, Paddy. X'll do, Paddy
Right fuckin state you were in last night, Paddy

Must be right proud of yourself, Paddy
I'll see you in court, Paddy.

Better pack your fuckin toothbrush, Paddy
Got toothbrushes in Ireland, Paddy?

4

Sunlight's like lime in me eyes
Tormented with horns an' engines an' drills

Not a copper to rub in me palms
Not a bull's where I am or where I'm off to

Not two straight thoughts runnin together
Brain whirlin like sand in a mixer

Shakes. I'm a holy show. I'm a disgrace.
I'm a walkin disaster.

A hole in the head

We were seen and not heard after your log broad thighs
strode over our nuisance of young ones in the hall,
clearing a path from the boot worn stairs through tricycles,
lego, toy soldiers, cabbage patch dolls,
waving an order to the quivering dew-nosed mongrel to "Get
Down Trixie" off the fire side of your one-piece suite.
Mothers gathered at the press, round the table, you cupped
your hands, gathered in the heat.

A horse of a man in your prime, you sat chomping great jowls
of bacon from the bone, swallowing glugs of Green Label.
Fed, you sat eyeing the canines of flames that leapt through
the scorched grate on the range you used as a table.
"Shush" for the Angelus, making the sign of the cross, a "be
quiet" for the six o clock news, a "put away that friggin ball".
Then upstairs. New shapes flickered to replace your looming
figure on the wall.

Navvy—your shanks swung down sledge hammers on tracks
from Manchester to Derby Town to Birmingham to Merseyside.
Living on site, playing twenty one, five hundred, draughts,
making craic for a couple of hours at night.
What was earned you sent it home except for Sean Nos in the
Shamrock, a couple of pints, a weekly five minutes of fame.

Nana scolded with the promise of the back of your hand
once Christmas came.
But you lugged bags of laughter back to Mitchel's, where six
or twelve months taller, the children rolled and scrambled at
your call,
and the little ones you loved but never knew would gaze in
guileless wonder at the shadow-shapes you projected on the wall.

Then postman at the door — dreaded telegraph panic-
staccato lines in black ink that usually ended with 'dead'.
A hammer-spark of iron had blasted out your right eye
and left a great hole in your head.
Sick-mans grey pittance of years under ceaseless Kerry
rain. Children gone to Boston, London, read and re-read
postcards piled to stacks,

And anything you could atall to fill the brain, walking the
mongrels, television, oul chat, a thousand torn and dusted
paperbacks.
Or spooked the visiting kids with a glass of teeth, rolled
out the mould on your tongue, called us up the stairs for a
surprise,
and there with belly-burst of laughter you would open out
a suitcase full of eyes.

The Toys

For Mary Smith

Cold Christmas nineteen fifty one
and the seven of us anchored
to the bottom of our luck
trippin over arms and legs
in the basement of a crumblin house
in a single dusty room
with no sunshine comin in.

Pullin the blankets tight around us
as ropes pull tight round tumblin men
for Tommy's only bits and pieces,
                              here and there,
                                        now and then.

Cold Christmas nineteen fifty one
and the children decide what the toys
their uncle carved from wood become.

Eddie's woof-woof turns
into Jimmy's rearin stallion
and when the two of them are gallivantin
Mary rides the desert on a camel.
The freckly yoke whose pointy nose
got blunted to a stub
will be doll-doll, trooper man, and Pinocchio
in turns.
Whose hands are glued to matchsticks
little drummer boy's or little drummer girl's,
or is it witch
                or wizard stirring spells?
The square wheeled motorcar
clunkin 'cross the table cloth—
zoomin in the hot rod or
cruisin sunny avenues in Hollywood?
The choo-choo steamin through the wildest wests

picks up a fly in Los Angeles
then later sails a letter to Australia,
delivers astronauts to Venus.
All the dreams
          my little girls and boys
                        can pull
                                    from painted wood!

He hadn't a start for the whole of January.
Though we kept the flame as best we could,
we were perishin'
for the whole of that spiteful month.
Then we ran out of coal,
we ran out of peat,
we ran out of logs,
we ran out of sticks and scraps and twigs.
St Brigid nearly froze our blood.

Do you know how it feels
to be chopped down like a wintry pine
to be lyin' on a bed of icy needles goin numb
from your branch-tips to your heart?
Do you know what it's like
to be suddenly sick of your stiffenin life
and wish
        that hell
              would burst
                        through the cracks in the floor
flare through the splits in the walls
and burn burn burn
everythin
you ought to be able to love ?

The toys were made of dreams and wood
and Oh
        how they burned.
                   I won't forget
                       and how to forgive
is what I have not learned.

Helicopter

A tomboy
always climbin trees and walls
scrobbin apples
robbin nests
the likes that got herself into trouble
with the priests and the nuns and the guards
and the people who counted their apples

She couldn't care less
not a bit
for all the warnins
for all the hidins from her father
even the scaldin print of my hand
across her back over and over
couldn't stop her
doin what she wanted to do

She just kept on climbin like a squirrel
a spider
a monkey
a great amusement for the soldiers in the barracks
who used to joke she was just what they needed in the army
with her long white legs
and her spindly fingers
and her hair cut short
and the way she could take all the knocks and the falls

like one of us the soldiers said
falls down and gets
straight back up again
dusts herself off and on to the next thing
like one of us

when the helicopters came
the commotion
the wind and the dust like one of Moses' plagues

there was no end to the pleadin
Mammy Mammy Mammy
Mammy please Mammy please Mammy
I'll be good forever
I'll be good till I die
Mammy please mammy please mammy please

so i let her off
i let her off for a ride with the soldiers
in the bastarin helicopter
not once or twice
but maybe a dozen times
that one of them called to the door for her
a dozen helicopter rides
with soldiers
dressed up to play war in their armour
a dozen times a little girl taken
away alone into the sky
a dozen times I let her
be held in the shadows
in the belly of that roarin monster

so hot
so cruel
so loud
so dark

not even god himself
nor all the electronic eyes
starin from heaven
could look
at what was goin on inside there

Turkey

evil in that house   the night's hollowness
wallpaper flaking from damp on the walls
echoes of coughing neon dogs
mumble of drunks shuffling home through the cold

shapes coiling in bedroom shadows
things scuttling shapelessly in draughts
something heavy in that house wanted out
something heavier again held it in

his childish whining in the witching hour
way past closing time at Nana's front door
across the room my asthmatic cousin
wept for shame   would not let him in

would not give the held hand   the mercy mouth
an ear for old harm   a quick burning fuck
he rapped and roared but turned again
the way he came   a flightless bird

hung a tree from his head in the park
three days swing in a pendulum's arc
the sense it makes to take revenge like that
to go and lock the whole damn world out

Bad Luck Story

Born with two turned eyes,
trophy-handle ears,
a pair of nostrils equine size,
and grew pimples, boils, hairy moles,
teeth that chipped, yellowed
and slanted like old tombstones.
To a father welting with an iron rod,
a mother's caustic hands
cracking red-raw skin, drawing blood.
One teen sister pregnant left behind,
the other a needle whore.
The butt of every broken misfortunate's joke
on an estate where no-one heard
above the screeching of their own four walls,
in a town not worth mentioning
on the edge of a retreating world.

Then pucked from big bully
to small bully in the classroom,
jerked around the schoolyard like a marionette.
Branded spastic, toolbox, thicko, shit-face
knacker, big ears, Frankenstein.
In a decade belonging to accountants and touts,
butchers and priests, what future?
Top of the world on a government scheme?
Frying on the wing for a hamburger team?

No
You stepped right out of those tracks,
sweet sixteen,
and mused a week, we'll say, on your design.
Shed,
Barrel,

Tube,
Mask,
Switch,
Gas,
This one thing you rounded off so handsomely.
This one thing you would not leave to accident.

At 14

What you left us all was mystery.
Disbelief by the sea.
So many strange introductions.
A church bell with no answer.
A packed church without a clue.
A priest in a hurry.
A blank sermon unmemorable as most.
Prayers no-one could believe in.
Your second-year classmates
An uncomfortable off-key choir. A closed coffin.

A hotel reception,
Soup or melon,
Then beef or chicken,
Or quiche for the vegetarians,
A sweet, coffee,
And an afternoon of beer
And light-hearted mourning.
Retreating waves gently pulsing,
An electric lawnmower droning all day
In the background.
Your mother gave a speech of thanks
Though her made up face was melting.
Your father pissed was shaking strangers
Hands and smiling.
Everyone agreeing it was less
Like a funeral than a wedding.
A day out by the sea in May,
Till the engine spluttered down and died.

And what were we left with,
Your sister's black-clad friends, five college transients,
Walking back along the shore from the hotel

To the bus-stop for Cork?
The tide far out into the Atlantic distance,
The sun's fierce orb strangled at the horizon,
Fierce light splintered in the rock-pools,
Fierce light shining through the cracks in the world.

A Theological Argument

For Erich Fried

Nameless in life
we died without names
because without a name
we couldn't live
and without a life
we couldn't die
and if we didn't die
we weren't killed
and if we weren't killed
no-one killed us
and if no-one killed us
there are no killers
and if there are no killers
then no-one can lie
about the lives
we didn't live
and the deaths
we didn't die

Tom Barry's ghost moves to Dublin

Who is there now that can remember
Our little intifada?
Here in the walled round city of the possible.
Here in the pale beyond the ditch of time.
In a time that should never have been,
In a petty Republic no more than a name.

There is no such thing as children.
Mothers and fathers I won't even mention,
Or the old men who used to sing and whistle
On the way to work,
Or the keeners who are long gone out of a job,
For who sees any sadness now in the going the flesh way.

Last week as I wandered round the bog
I saw the last telling ruin bulldozed to the ground.
Or the doors nailed shut,
Or the windows painted black.
Nor a well or a tinker's horse or a sloe-bush to be found.
The whole shaggin country's a golf course.
Them and their men made of bronze.

Well I tell you now it's a sad day
When there's not a sinner left around
To haunt with hope.
When even the ghosts give up
The ghost
And move to Dublin.

my country

What is wrong with me?
my country is not just a comic book lie
my country is a free country

in my country we
have established beyond challenge
the traditions and structures of democracy

no-one would dare put handcuffs on dogs
caught messing with fences

pigs attaching crazy signs to lampposts
are generally left to their own devices

not a word is ever said to foxes
doling out treacherous leaflets in batches

nor are ants denied the right
to carry ten times their body weight

pigeons too are lucky to live here
having plenty to eat and many addresses

train driving cats with tobacco stained whiskers
can do anything they like at the weekend

any bunch of confederate pests can host
an assembly of rats in a basement

crows amassed on overhead wires
may deem themselves a parliament

the mice in the hot press get friendly policemen
if hosting a rave or a champagne reception

best of all our friendly president, a seal,
talks to each without exception

and so I must practise being happy
as I circle the streets of our capital city
disguised as myself on a bike

for even our statues of virgins are allowed
to cry and bleed and move around
in any direction they like

Skinny-dipping, White's Cove.

For Richard

We had plenty of fags,
cans, matches,
the stereo was working.

We lit nightlights
and set them in the sand
between shells
and fossil-patterned stones.

Between us
we got a joint together,
passed it round.

We lit sparklers,
set off fireworks,
the night had many colours.
The breeze was alive.

We had leaves in our hair
and stuck to our clothes
from the forest.
Huge birds squalled inside sea mist.

We stripped off; first one,
then the rest
ran whooping and hooting and howling
into the bay.

I was worried about the Guards
sneaking up on us,
but fuck the Guards. Yes, fuck them.

Braced in the water, ghosts
fled my blood and swam away,
I forgot the tug of time and doom,
I forgot.

Ashore we couldn't find
where we had flung our underwear
so we left it there among the odds and ends.

Then up the concrete steps,
iron echoes on the railway bridge,
the slow ascent to heavy-lidded dawn.

What old man puffing after
a cocker spaniel,
what early morning jogger
found our leavings lying in that cove?

Fragments abandoned,
relics of a vanished culture.

Migrants March, Genoa, July 19, 2001

For Carlo Giuliani

After the warm embrace of a cheerful revolutionary monk
from Salerno I get to chatting in some kind of pidgin

to an Iraqi man who has pedalled all the way here
from Paris on a rickshaw.

'Cead Mile Failte', our ten word Italian lexicon,
my leaving cert pass French, salut, comment tu apples?
The universal bits of English like 'War' and 'McDonalds'.

Then
our conversation's broken up
by the roar that meets a band of Kurds arriving
in Piazza del Kennedy behind the yellow banner of the PKK.
And then eighty cyclists hooting
and whooping in from Berlin.

The slogans surging up the back of fifty thousand throats
to greet them in our provisional republic.

Free-Free Kurdistan.
So-So Solidarité.
A- Anti- Anti-capitalista.
Un altro mondo é possible.
Noi siamo tutti clandestini.

A language we all understand.
Is there any such thing as Ireland?

Death of a Handyman

Trapped for an hour in the motorway traffic.
Morning Ireland prattling on about our unusual weather,
their experts sifting through the morning's tray of fresh disasters—
infants being scythed in Gaza, being stoned at a Belfast school.
Our small talk stretches taut and snaps;
after three weeks of rising hopes
there's blood again in your stool.

       *

Sell house sell van,
sell tools, move on,
downsize, two rooms will have to do,
Now what?
Now who?
Now where to?

       *

All their gardens clamping shut
behind their high electric gates
while ulcers gnaw your colon
and you learn to shit through plastic tubes
wearing nappies like a new born
and to queue queue queue queue
and wait wait wait wait
to fill in never ending forms
pleading thin cold mercies of the state

       *

The M1 thaws.
We deal slogans.
One Day At A Time,
Easy Does It,

Think Think Think
This Too Shall Pass.
Snap and snap and snap and snap.

*

Zooming through Stillorgan
towards the next appointed task—
reconstructing half an acre in Foxrock.

*

Without asking,
I pick the Big Blue Book from off the sill
and leafing through discover
that its not the Big Blue Book I mean
but is instead *The Book of Mormon.*
I fold it shut and sit it back again,
without asking.

*

Sculpting beech to suit the lady's privacy
binning those damned discolouring leaves
hacking the loathsome glut of weeds
snapping the muscle thick fibres of vines
burning maggots snails and slugs
from their trenches tunnels under rocks
slimy bastards watch them writhe
bombed with phosphorous and lime

*

Hours we bend and heave and drag,
hours snipped and tugged and piled and bagged
hours sweating in this strange November heat
and hardly halt to share a word or catch a breath
save pitying an out of season bumblebee

heading south across the garden drowsily
flying by next year's uncompleted map
in a drunk erratic droning zig zag
hovering over the flowerless stems
snouting their unborn blooms for pollen
then dropping rapidly to earth
and driving its sting into the dirt;
lured by the lying sun from its hibernal rest
springtime in the winter confusing it to death.

*

I light a cigarette,
rest against the garden trampoline,
build me a thousand new prisons
I'll fill them with my raging dream.

*

Beneath a sheared bush
two sparrows peck at the dust
then peck each other.

*

I want to run
out of this half
conquered garden
I want to leave
the dogged weeds
to groping on
to leave them sucking
unnatural light
out of this odd late
sun.

Driving Home From Derry, Feb 3rd 2002.

For Catherine

After the hours retracing
Bloody Sunday's route with thirty thousand,
from the Creggan Height right down to the basin of the Foyle,
through all those ordinary, downtrodden, every-streets to Free
Derry Corner.
After the speeches, the clapping, the marching bands, the mourning,
the silence, the wind in the flags; after the names were joined—
Derry, Palestine, Afghanistan—
time came for five to hurry back before the frozen road
would stay us for the night.

Out we drove towards Aughnacloy
past the union colours painted on the kerbstones,
past 'FUCK THE BRITS' and 'UP THE UDA',
past the watchtowers and the listening posts,
past election snipers and billboard hunger strikers,
on over a sudden blizzard's leftover slush and ice,
on and on towards the invisible line,
on towards the republic of signs.

When "See that there" said Brid, the driver, to Zack from Gaza,
jabbing through the windscreen at the Greco-Roman night.
"See that there, that's Orion. See the three bright stars across,
that's his belt
and see the two small ones down on the left, that's his sword
and see his big head and shoulders, see them?"

"Aha" said Zack behind her — half-asleep and dreaming perhaps
of diving as a child into the starlit Nile to catch a fish between
bare hands
or of the Gaza stars his father fished beneath
and of the stars his father's father saw before him.

And in the back seat our heads lolled at the frost–glittering stars,
seeking out *Hercules, Cassiopeia , Perseus, Andromeda...*

And in the back seat I got to dreaming
about how when the war is over,
when the curse of blood and soil is done,
we'll both lie naked and brave under a starlit sky
stretched on the fine sand of a phosphor-shimmering bay
somewhere out there in the wide world,
and how one by one, we'll tear the gods down off the sky
and hang new names for the constellations, you and I.

What I am seeing

What am I seeing now
when I look at a tree
standing alone
in the middle of a country field?

Not the strength to bend straight in the terrible weather.
Not an indomitable will to live.

Now I am seeing the absent forest,
the undecided emptiness,
the cut down things.

Explanations of War

See all those bright lights whizzing around in the sky—
They are only the stars throwing a party.
And the shaking you feel beneath you,
The shaking that jars your teeth and your bones—
That is only the way the earth dances.
And the bangs and roars, the cracks and blasts and booms—
These are only the sounds of little spirits tuning their instruments.
And the horrible wailing that rises and falls, rises and falls
above the buildings—
That is only the rooftops shrieking their envy that they cannot
fly off.
And the high fires that climb above the rooftops—
These are the rejoicing souls of our city flying to heaven.
And the black clouds of smoke blotting the beautiful woman
of the moon—
These are our dark acts evaporating.
And you my child, lying still in my arms,
Lying stiff as a mould of ancient clay,
You my child, you are only sleeping.

Road Map No Road

Because there was nothing left of a child
In the photograph on the front cover of the Irish Times
On Friday June 13th 2003

Save what the man in the foreground
Of the perennial southern crowd
Had raised in his fists to the sun—

A fire scarred plastic bottle
And one tiny blackened shoe,

I drew a hand.
I drew a matchstick man.
I drew a map.

Love

For H.G

She rushes screaming from the sparkling sea
the little girl
    all gone
Her father on all fours
laying out the chicken,
hummus, salad, olives, bread,
drooping belly
tender to the broiling sand
warmth
her two brothers start to kick a ball into the sun
laughter
soon as she finishes chapter 12 her older sister will dip in
waves
her uncle snoozing underneath his hat and beard
peace
Her mother with the overheated baby at her breast
song

Peace hat beard chicken laughter uncle breast baby hum-
mus mother nails warmth bread sister sun ball waves
brothers belly father picnic sand song salad love

    all gone

        the sea
        rushes screaming
        from the little girl

An Only Child.

i.m. Zhao Liu Tao murdered in Dublin in January 2002.

I had my grandfather's mouth.
In famine he was told to thrive on hunger.
He wouldn't swallow it.
They cut his tongue out.

I had my father's eyebrows.
They arced like blackbird's wings
and nearly touched across his brow.
He kept his head down.

I had my mother's lips.
She sang true songs of long ago.
Now my lips are blue,
she sews her's up in grief.

I was last in a line,
shouldering well the hope of many.
I was an only child,
bearer of a name's eternity.

When they burst my skull with an iron bar
they murdered so well, so often.
They killed my father, my mother
and all before and after for ever and ever.

Like a stream vanished in a drought
we are gone to a place without laughter,
a place without children,
a place of endless silence.

When I came here only wanting
to open my mouth,
when I came here only wanting
to learn how to speak.

The Longest Queue

This a story I heard from a friend
who heard it from an Iraqi engineer
who fled away to Ireland
from bomb clouds and anthrax
in the rain and queues for food.
He rings home once a month
to speak to his dying mother
and to hear news of his family and neighbours.
That night he told the story he
had asked after a friend of his,
a doctor with two beautiful daughters
and a young boy.
His mother went silent, darkly silent,
fifty pence gobbling silent.
A couple of months ago this doctor
lost his job and was left to
live on government rations,
not a lot to go on by all accounts
and anyway he owed some money
to a smuggler for getting
his mother over the border to Jordan.
Faced with starvation he improvised
and sent his two beautiful daughters
one eighteen, the other fifteen
out to sell their bodies,
and his ten year old son to shine shoes and beg.
Financially it worked out,
they'd even set some money aside.
But the man was broken hearted,
not to speak of how his children must have felt.
So the man decides to cook a chicken for his family.
He goes to queue in the marketplace.
It's a short queue since chickens
cost six weeks average wages.
Then the slightly longer line for vegetables
and the four hours waiting for bread.

Maybe he thinks to himself
that the only thing longer than this bread queue
is the waiting list at the coffin-makers.
Next day is some kind of religious feast
so he tells his kids to be at the dinner table at seven.
He's got a surprise for them.
While preparing the chicken
he searches through his leftover medicines
for a suitable poison
to inject into the breast and leg meat.
The daughters and the son arrive in time
and they sit around the table chatting,
faking good humour for the good of their father,
like they always do.
The doctor divides the meat among them,
a breast and leg for himself,
a breast for the eldest daughter,
a leg for the younger,
a leg and two wings for the son.
He gestures to his son to share out the vegetables.
They say their prayers quickly, mouths watering.
Since none of them has eaten meat for
months and months they take
their time, chewing each mouthful
with the relish reserved for a luxury,
rolling it round with their tongue,
squeezing the taste out with their teeth.
The boy asks for more and gets it.
They do not talk while they are eating.
They concentrate on the taste and the smell.
The doctor is a subtle and a skillful cook,
his children notice nothing unusual,
he gives nothing away with sighs or tears.
They do not even notice themselves dying.
In a few minutes they are all dead.
They have joined the longest queue of all.
I hope this isn't a true story
but I'd say it probably is.

In the weeping room, Baggot Street

At length the tears
were dripping out of everything.
When her kettle whined
like an electric cat
the walls and the ceiling cried.
Her cup and her bowl wept in her throat.
Her tap leaked the same fat brass tear over and over.

Through the mesh she watched the red horizon weeping stars
and saw the moonface weeping ice.
At dawn the panes shone with the tears of the wind
and the grass outside with the tears of the frost.
Beneath the window
the gutter continuously sobbed.

From sun-down till sun-up
men with roadmaps
were queuing for appointments
to weep in her mouth.

On the Television
the newsreaders sat on their silver combs and screeched
and all the cartoon superheroes
were speechless with grief.

When they gave her a paper bag
filled with broken crayons
she scrawled enormous teardrops on the wall
and locked the images of people
who cried in her nostrils inside them .

One night her tights wept faces
her beads wept shadows
her high heels wept beetles

and when an old atlas fell from the shelf
exposing itself
it sprayed meaningless tears of dust.

Her ultimate cry
arrived in the shape of two clipped wasps
pushing
through a yellow machine in the door.

They buzzed insanely at her eyes
then burst her head open
like a bag of fish.

Then the dancing triangular woods in the distance
keened themselves out of existence
and streams gushed from the Wicklow hills
desperate for cliffs.

Holding Chirac's hand in Temple Bar

The angels have fallen.
They are not of God
And not of the Devil
Or of themselves
They are of neon
They are of strobelight
They are of ink and dye
They are of rubber and plastic and fur
Or they are simply here
Walking the cobbles
In Temple Bar
Drunk and stoned
On a Friday night
With gel and stillettos,
Tattoos and thigh-boots
Belly-tops and wonderbras
Wigs and masks.
Some have stuck-on tails
Some bunny ears
Some leprechaun hats
Some plastic arses
But their mouths have no faces
Their singing is senseless
And the cobbles absorb and forget
Their laughter and sighs
Their urine and vomit
While ould orators' ghosts
Are beaten down and bleed
Into the cracks of the street.
Around the corner
On Dame Street
Near the Green
I saw three Muslim girls
Wearing the hijab.
More power to them.

Shelley leaving Dublin

For Paul O Brien

I went down among the mob and shouted
loudly as I could but no-one heard.
I chased all through the drunken neighbourhoods
past huts that leaned like rotten teeth but they took no heed.
Though I rained my pamphlets down from balconies
and dropped my address in their hoods
no seething wind blew up to show that they had understood.
Perhaps they could not read. Perhaps I hadn't spelt the
proper words.

I swallowed more than claret dining at this crow-shat city's
tables of fireside enlightenment to speak out on their behalf,
but won neither shillings nor commitment,
though raised many the fatherly chuckle, the patronising laugh:
'When you get old you'll sup and puff like us,
you'll make no dent in God or nature's given world by
raising such a fuss'.

I pleaded in sheets of letters to the London set
for public words and an Irish vote in parliament. But men
whose minds fired on the incandescence of the French events
and, in the dawning rage of sans culottes,
saw the chrysalis of nearly perfect love,
have flown from youth and with it all that's news. Some even
hymn the church, the generals, the government,
stand side by side with Castlereagh, praise aristocratic shite
as sugared cake.

And so I've failed. The many headed monster's still sleeping
deep within it's sightless cave. I need retreat and confess
I'm more than slightly burnt. But this I've learnt: I was
not wrong

To plant the flag of fire among the mob, but one man's voice is not enough,
one cry, however like the nightingales, dies amidst the clamour, cut off.
Minds like mine must seek proliferation. Therefore,
I propose an association.

Excerpt from Reflections on Shannon

Silence
A minute's silence
A three-minute silence
Silent silent bloody silence
Silence in the courtyard
Silence in the street
Silence at the warport
Silence at the embassies
Silence in the parliaments
Silence in the offices
Silence in the nightclubs
Silence in the factories
Silence from the journalists

What the fuck is silence?

Is it a prayer?
Is it womb?
Is it a ticket?
Is it an art-form?
Is it an emporer?

I ask you again
What the fuck is silence;
And who has ever heard
The dead requesting it?

    ***

I am confused
I have been to a meeting
now I'm feeling murderous, suicidal
suicidally murderous
murderously suicidal

What do I mean 'I feel'?
What do I mean 'I'?

Fuck off with your questions I'm cranky
I'm sick of myself
and I'm sick of humanity
I'd blow the earth up if I could
I'd dig down to the core of the world and explode.

What if the 'I' could be shattered?
What if the me could be burning daggers in an instant
flying in all directions?
Where would I plant the me?
Where would I set the me off?

The thought occurs
that according to the orthodox view
the universe is the result of an explosion
is that explosion ongoing

Time
space
matter
stretching
bending
colliding
flying apart
all created by
all existing in
the explosion at the origin

so ourselves
and all we do
is part of the explosion
since the big bang isn't over
and things are flying apart

and if there is a god
as in a creator
as even Stephen Hawking
seems at times to be suggesting
then she was a bomber
perhaps she was a suicide bomber?
This neurosis is quickening
one mad thought follows another
what if
I mean the formulas do suggest
everything is possible
everything is happening
that in the infinity of universes
nothing whatsoever is avoidable
and all is redeemed
so there is no death
only every possible action
every possible combination
shapes and sizes
arrangements and re-arrangements
heads where your feet should be
balls at the end of your fingers
necks stretched thin as wires
little fingers fatter
like in a hall of mirrors going on forever

somewhere else I am my own happy mother
Rosa Luxembourg is still alive
there is no *Guernica*
no-one has ever heard of the Swastika
somewhere else all the smashed eggs are being put back
together again
all the broken children are being remade
the drunks have stopped drinking and taken up yoga
the boys have stopped crashing their cars

foxes escape unhurt from their traps
and the snow is no longer spotted with blood

so it's all good
fun just experiment
so what
if
going by these rules of engagement
I were to blow myself up?

Would that make me a God?
What kind of universe would my explosion make?

***

Dublin
ATGWU Hall Middle Abbey Street
7.30 pm
Friday Dec 3rd 2004

Can I be happy if others suffer?
Can I be true if the world is a lie?
Can I be good if I allow evil to rule over me?

What is my life worth if life is worth less than nothing?
What is my death to the deaths of thousands?
What is one bull in a stampede?

Is it only by offering my death
that I can prove I am alive?
Is it by stopping sensation
I can prove that I feel?

Love is the proof of the objective existence of others

***

Shalom Doctor Faisal
Shalom Shalom

Slide One

Boy nine years old
has one arm
one leg
one eye
black scabs
blood black as oil
thick stitches

Smashed genitals
Smashed genitals

Slide Two

Girl seven
no arms
no legs
shaved head
scorched eyebrows
smiling at the camera
died a half an hour later

Slide Three

Street in ruins
crater pocked
after cluster bomb
heaps of concrete

mangled wire
steaming limbs
unexploded ordnance
bright orange
looks so innocent
shaped like a baby's rattle
or some other kind of toy

Slide Four

In background
hospital
with collapsed roof
in foreground
four male doctors

Two of them now dead
one sniped at
one exploded

We knew the American snipers
were getting bored
when they started shooting
at stray dogs

The hunger striker sings his death

This is my body
my pale body
my hairy body
my stinking body
my body with its moles and leaks
my body with its scars and sores and sweats
my body with its itches and its aches
my longing body
my weeping body
my body whipped
my body bruised my body crushed
my spat on body my pissed on body
my punched and kicked and electrocuted body
my shivering starving body in a cell

Surrounded by bars and floodlights and grilles
watchtowers and gates and electronic locks
walls inside walls inside walls inside walls
corners where light is flung like a swift axe
shadows pregnant with nooses and saws
barbed wire puzzles, riddles of broken glass
snares of bayonets, mazes of steel pincers and claws

guarded by needles in pipes arrows in clocks
and eight-legged poisonous cameras
by mikes attached to Beetles
by double-shifting psychopaths and cannibals
drunken teenage marksmen on the roofs
german shepherds laced with speed
stallions with serrated hooves

besieged by self reloading magazines
rapid fire repeating headlines
morning artillery and main evening shells
battalions of experts in think thanks

heroic newscasters riding on elephants
khaki battalions of correspondents
the black watchers of Reuters and the BBC

stormed by blowtorches, fists and boots
by electric wires and twine and LSD
by white noise and burning cigarette butts
by a black hole pointed at my mother's head
by great white sharks circling my Dad
by a mushroom cloud painted over my wife
by tidal waves aimed at my kids

here is my body
my famished and shrivelling body
where I am making my last and unbreakable stand
where slowly, by the ebbing minute
by the shrinking hour
by the days pouring sand in the canyon of my mouth
by the days piling silt in the river of my mouth
by the days spilling lava in the valley of my mouth
I am lightening
I am losing gravity
I am loosening the ballast of my flesh
I am ungluing myself from the spools of my eyes
and untying the knots of my hearing and touch
and slipping the hooks of my taste and my smell
I am winding out of pain's net
I am winding out of the shrouding of sense
and I am going down to the very core of myself
to be safer from their tortures
than at the centre of a sun
safer than a cave in an ocean trench
safer than ice in mountain's heart

and there beyond the blind horizon of events
in a prophet's cell
in a house of pure light
I am giving birth to my invincible death.

Dying for Ireland

I am already well past grieving myself
by the time
I finally get to this morning,
but cringe at thoughts of my father
at the front door explaining
my mother's Antigonian wailing.

Six weeks without sleep,
three without solids,
a classic lack of attention
to basic self-caring tasks
like washing and shaving,
and the latest phase—
diabolic—
the babble ceaselessly prompting.

Are enough for me to be pleased
at the prospect
of draining
away on the bed
with bloodied muscles twitching,
my fingers and eyes
deliriously trembling.

In true Irish martyr fashion
I've decided not to give a warning.

Moments before a murder

You could tell I had a criminal intent
by the carefree way I hopped and skipped
across four streaming lanes of cars and trucks
as a man might dance an Irish jig
through the galloping heart of a stampede
and by how, like a child on a green being tugged by a kite
much too quickly up a slope
I gamboled up the concrete steps
entering the Eurostudent dorm
on my tippy toes

Then when I stood in reception
dashing mustard from the flap of my kebab
onto the cool blue tiles
(not to mention the provocation of the mayonaisse
dribbling from my chin onto my shirt and my shorts
my raggy sandals and my unmatched socks)
it was obvious that I was gone
quite villainously mad

Christ I hadn't shaved or slept or changed my jocks
or cut my hair or brushed my teeth or washed
or done anything but sigh and weep
and drink hot milk and clench my teeth
for going on a month
and now some fucking dam inside had burst
and what was flowing out
unstoppably
was laughter

Laughter gushing from my tongue
laughter tumbling from my belly
laughter gouting from my guts

as deliriously as the blood
jets from a hacked artery
I tell you every bone every organ
every cell in my body was giddy
I had to drop to my knees on the floor
I had to lock my hands to my mouth
I had to press my lips to the tiles

but the laughter kept on flooding out invincibly
laughter echoing and echoing and echoing and echoing
echoing up six marble flights of stairs
echoing round the building's underworld of Egyptian
cleaning ladies, Congolese janitors, Macedonian chamber-
maids, Moroccan watch sellers
echoing under the locked doors of Albanians and Slavs,
their secret refuges
echoing over a Polish biophysicist carrying a bag of
poisonous fish
echoing past an Irish dipso walking hand in hand with a
Nigerian princess
echoing through a debate on human rights between a
Scotswoman and a Portuguese
echoing at the Finnish breakfast on the balcony of bread
and smokey ham and cheese
echoing by a game of poker played by Germans Swiss and
Swedes
laughter laughter laughter laughter
echoing echoing echoing echoing
like a tannoy announcing the end of all tears
like a train of hooting howling ghouls
all in bententangled stitches at the world

When I raised myself back up again
I was dizzy with the sudden weightlessness
I was as light as a helium balloon
and I found that I could moonwalk up the stairs

so I bounced from landing up to landing
as if the twelve step flights were little red hillocks on mars
which was some relief
for a man who had been walking
with a stoop for six long weeks
who had been crooked underneath
the weight of his own coffin
It's hard to carry a coffin on your own

But this bouncing trip upset the Albanian heiress
I was in love with
and she quickly scurried upwards
her rattletail beating out a rapid rhythm on the steps
to report the incident to the office of the minister her brother
who held the east and the west as having different
and totally incompatible histories of love

But it wasn't long and I was over the loss
and when I twice belched loudly
in the direction of a passing ring
of popular guys and beautiful girls
someone surely should have phoned the police
and if they had come and arrested me
and took a little peek inside my head
before I'd achieved my chamber
the nice policemen would have seen
how comical how farcical
this whole world really is to the dead

And really I think they would have had problems
ever again breaking the faces of students
or raising those you're-so-intelligent chuckles
at the bitternonsensical comments of judges
or even getting themselves up out of bed
for they'd have seen how everything everything everything is
just a string of oozy melting beads

in an almost endless chain
strung together in a river
that's pouring all the way
round the almost interminable bends
from the suicidal bang at the origin
to the last screech of light
being sucked
into an eye
at the end

But then the nice policemen did not come
for with all the phones
no-one thought to ring them up
and anyways I now realise
the crime was never dying by my choice
but was the pure unfiddled-with release
I got for giving in to death

For nairy a roaring ocean full of stout
nor a moony mountain lake of laudanum
nor twenty sheets of Timmy Leary's LSD
nor an artic lorry loaded with cocaine
nor even fucking your most flexible lover
all night on the purest of E
could reach that supersensational peak
that complete unassailable high
that I had received from death
in return
for agreeing to die.

Of Attis and Cybele

(Carmen 63, Gaius Valerius Catullus)

For Ronan Sheehan

"The screeching furies rode the ancient winds
And lashing out with glass-tipped tails
Drove Attis and his twisted crew
Across interminable days.
Astride a mile long iron deck
Attis drilled his skulking ranks
Through heaving seas of piss and blood.
They painted flags of jagged teeth,
And with raggy scraps of napalmed skin
Polished up their mercenary steel.

When at last they pitched upon a midnight shore,
A mountain's shadow-blackened hoof,
Attis ranked his thousand brothers all together
Along the dark and loathsome sands, and standing
Proud upon a rock before their gazing lines
He roared: "Before the creeping dawn
Strips this shady mountain bare
We're going to gain the mountaintop,
And be writhing joyously, out of our minds,
Like nests of incense-addled snakes,
In the courtyard of my mother, Cybele's, fort.
And here before we start, before you all I'll prove my
mother-love,
I'll tear my own balls off for MOTHER DEATH, for
MOTHER DEATH".
So down he bent, and with the sharpened blade of a bayonet
Sliced out his tree of life, root and all.
Attis brayed like an electrocuted mule,
Attis bled like a slit-throated bull,
Then watched his brothers emulate.

Men no more, trailing dark red rivulets,
In which the strangest stalks took root,
They charged as one mad rushing troop
Into the forest's deeper gloom,
On and up towards the mother lair, the mountaintop.
All night they trampled down the ferns,
All night they scrambled over rocks,
All night they tore past thorns and grizzled bark,
All night they hollered, sang and screamed,
Banged out tunes with hollowed shins on tambourines,
Till their lungs were raw and quit
And their amphetamine insanity was spent.
Then tripping up and staggering round
Like squads of wet-brain, park-bench drunks,
They fell to earth, and took the land of nod.

Between two steaming mouldy rocks
Attis curled up on the crawling forest floor
And dribbled, dreaming, on his mother's breasts,
A dream that flushed his madness clear.

Attis awoke. Sun-fire and shadow danced across his skin,
Dawn song warbled from the canopy.
The air and everything within was pine-pure and glassy-still.
His mind was fresh and clean,
An empty glass, poison free.
But quickly flooding guilt took hold, regret, and fear,
And spying the boiling rusted scab that clamped
His midriff, a putrid leaf from a tree of rot,
Attis set to abandoning his groaning seedless crew
And fled back cock-less to the shore.

Across a white sea of fire he stared,
Across an endless sea of burnished skulls, he stared,
And pleaded for the fathering of home.

Where he could spend himself in slot machines as old,
Where he could train again his hounds to tear the snouts
From other hounds,
Where he has bitten earlobes off with glee,
And guffawing stamped in jaws with studded heels.
Attis cried: "Oh take me to the streets of living pain—
enduring things,
The streets my father rules with cane and buckle, boot
and blade,
For there's nothing here but weeds to slash,
Just vermin hides to pierce and skin".

A hundred yards away, shrouded in an arboreal mist,
Flanked by lizards, cobras, lions
A guarding coterie of unnameable, phantasmagoric beasts,
Cybele marked her only son's betrayal,
And spinning in a fearsome rage,
She ordered out her fiercest brute: " Scatter Attis from the shore,
Harry his heels to deepest woods till he is lost
And whimpering, and roams alone for evermore".
The lion sprung, and Attis fled, dripping blood, into the
darksome wood.
Slithering branches shut the darkness in behind him.
So were Attis and his brothers trapped,
So still, deathless and undone,
They roam those vulture taunted woods".

Oh Mother Death
Old time whining coffin queen
Queen of bombs that look like toys
Queen of toys that look like bombs
Queen of Kings and Presidents
Queen of maiming
Queen of depletion
Queen of rendition
Queen of hoods and executions

Queen of absence
Queen of fragments
Queen of disappearance
Queen of the swarms of red-hot nails
Glittering
Phosphorescent
Corrosive
Flame-engulfing queen
Silver haired and shadow browed
Blue tongued and bloody eyed
Your needle crown
Your dress of shards
Your yellow breathe
Your crooked teeth
Your deadly stare
Your pallid flesh
Your frigid limbs
Your pus filled veins
I hate you
I hate you
I will not be your lover
I plug my ears to the
Lure of your moan
I refuse your embrace
I will not be your lover
Keep the white dust of your knock from my door
Keep the stamp of your black lips for someone else.

Inchadoney

For My Uncle Garrett

I have run my heart down
to a fading blue line

where headlands infrequently erupt
like cells beneath a microscope

I hope to be drifting as salt
till the sun stops pumping light

to be slowly devouring this coast
the invisible teeth in the brine